RUTH JEREMIAH CORNWALL

Order this book online at www.trafford.com
or email orders@trafford.com

Most Trafford titles are also available at major online book retailers.

Printed in the United States of America.

ISBN: 978-1-4907-3441-5 (sc)
ISBN: 978-1-4907-3443-9 (hc)
ISBN: 978-1-4907-3442-2 (e)

Library of Congress Control Number: 2014907550

Trafford rev. 06/02/2014

 www.trafford.com

North America & international
toll-free: 1 888 232 4444 (USA & Canada)
fax: 812 355 4082

Throughout my life growing up I had faced many difficult times, but I always know that God's grace sustained me and showed me love.

Born the youngest of eight, five boys and three girls, my Mom and Dad took very good care of us.

They showed us how to be caring, independent and protective of one another and even though it was a love that was never spoken, it was definitely showed in many ways.

My parents taught us how to pray, brought us up to trust in God and to be thankful for everything, everyday for whatever it might be, big or small.

As children we believe that when our parents are correcting us from doing something wrong, that they are doing us harm, but until we grow up to become adults ourselves and begin to make choices of our own and sometimes makes the wrong choice in life we realize later why they are directing us through life.

God has kept me strong throughout my journey because of his love for me and I know it.

I was bullied, teased and humiliated while growing up. In elementary school, I was called soldier because of the way I walked; I don't know why because I never thought I walked like a soldier. They would follow me and walked behind me with marching sounds while shouting the word soldier. I was constantly being teased for my last name and when I got to high school I was then teased for both first and last name, non of those times made me happy because I felt ridicule, sad and humiliated all the time, so I would shy away from being a social butterfly, just a few friends. I remember getting into a fight one day when my classmate pulled me by the back of my hair. That was the first and last time I've ever fought, because my Mom found out about it ;the most I remember her saying to me after every lash was. "I sent you to school to learn your ABC not to fight, I sent you to school to learn to read and write not to fight." I got a good whooping that day. Oh boy, did I ever learned my lesson ; I learned that fighting does not solve problems it makes things worse.

But that didn't stop me from becoming mindfully strong.

I was thrown out from my first communion class by the priest and the Nun because I started going to another church with my oldest sister.

When my sister got baptized into the Seventh-day Adventist Church, I started going with her on Saturdays and sometimes with my Mom on Sundays. The priest found out I was also going to church on Saturdays by a parishioner, so at the next session of our communion class he asked me to sit in front the middle of the class with both himself and the Nun facing the kids.

The class was sitting in a half circle, it felt as though I was in the high court.

Then he started asking me some Questions; His first question was, "What church does your mother go to?"

I said, "Catholic."

"What church does your father go to?" I said, "evangelical."

"Who do you go to church with on Saturday?" I said, "my sister." He then said to me you should be going to church with your mother because she brought you into this world.

He said, "get out of this class and don't come back anymore, so I did. Ridiculed and humiliated but still strong.

As an adult, it didn't get much easier, there's always some rough spots in life, it sometimes feels as though everything is going the wrong way. You get blindsided by the ones you trust and betrayed by the one you loved, but then you find yourself in that peaceful place called reality soul searching and it brings out the best in you. Your spiritual being within you gets connected with the holy spirit and it's amazing what you can overcome once you let it guides you.

In 1998 I was living in Brooklyn New York at the time, I had a dream that night and in that dream I saw the heavens open, bright blue sky filled with angels and I heard music playing, the song that was playing is he's coming, coming, he's coming soon I know. I didn't tell anyone because I didn't want them to think otherwise like I'm going off my mind, I only thought to myself that I need to start going back to church before its too late, because I haven't been going to church for a while, so I started going back to church.

February of 2013 that dream came back to me only this time it was different, I saw three Angels at first so I went into the building where I was working and called one of the resident out to show her and when we got back outside there were more Angels in the sky and the face of Jesus, the next day I went to work I told that resident my dream, her respond was," I knew there's something special about you." Two weeks later I dreamt that I was preaching to a congregation, the church was located at a plaza, as I was preaching I happen to look out through the window on the left and saw a woman been blown by a straight wind that was blowing just directly at her, she was trying to hold on to a pole and about four or five people was trying to hold onto her so she wouldn't be blown away, I went over and said just lay your hand on her back like this, with a gentle touch at her back she was able to stay calm and the wind subsided. I then heard a voice saying to me in a very clear voice, Go preach the gospel. Are all those dreams connected? I believe so.

God has a plan for all of us we just have to be still and listen so we can hear his voice.

Proverbs 3 : 5-6 says, "Trust in the Lord with all thine heart and lean not unto thine own understanding, In all thine ways acknowledge him and he shall direct your path.

Gods plan for me is to spread his love to others through poetry and to inspire every heart, let them know that he is real, we should never doubt his presence just because something bad happen but instead we should trust in him more and more, so our faith will grow stronger in him.

Satan wants us to believe that there is nothing to live for ; but he is wrong, let him know he is so wrong.

God is in control and he always will be until he returns again, he is a gracious and loving God who cares for his children, we need not to turn our eyes away from him.

Satan is very deceiving, he tries to make the wrong things seem to be right and then he plants the seeds of hatred, animosity and anger in the hearts of humans, so they would start living in disbelief, losing faith and hope in the things that are true, making many people have doubts in their hearts and minds of who God really is.

I was inspired to write this book when I saw how much my life has changed despite all the obstacles and tough times I've been through. When we pray and ask God for change, we should realize that change does not always come automatically but we should be willing to give up the old self and open up to a new beginning inside ourselves, our thoughts should be free, free from everything that is impure and let God take control of the situation: Believe, have faith and trust in God, ask God's forgiveness for our selfish thoughts and sinful words that may have come out from our mouths, look within ourselves and forgive one self and then we will be able to forgive others, for when the bible says forgive seventy times seventy, I believe it means being able to forgive always and let God do the rest.

To all those who read this book, think of how God is great and his works are wonderful, let his holy spirit fill your hearts with love and kindness to one another. For he is the majestic one, the one and only living God who through perilous times will open his arms and comfort us and show us that it's only through miracles wonders can happen.

I left home one morning on my way to work, that morning I had such a heavy burden weighing down on me. I was so stressed out and feeling really down, it felt as though everything was closing up on me, so much to think about at the same time my blood pressure was just elevating. When I got to the parking lot at work, I thought I was going to passed out my head was pounding, my whole body felt weak all I can hear my mind telling me is to read your bible. As always I carry my bible with me in the car, I opened it and the first page I got to was Psalm 27; I read the whole chapter the words were just speaking to me it made me felt at ease I said, "this is what I needed to hear, thank you Lord Jesus." I prayed in the car and I asked God to give me strength that day, when I open my eyes I can only think of how God is good and he is always there for me. As I walked through the building that morning I can feel a change in me my head felt better, my body was stronger and my mind was clearer.

Sometimes it's very hard for me to talk about the things that bothers me or personal problems to others, I always try to fix things myself if I can, but that morning I realized I couldn't, I couldn't do it all alone so I confided in a friend, it was like dropping a heavy load off from me. By talking to her, she let me know that there are many people in the same situation like me and even worse, so I shouldn't be ashamed to talk about it, even though others may do you wrong by their actions you should never be afraid. She prayed with me during our lunch break. I went home that afternoon and I said, "Lord you have sent her in my life for a reason and that is to remind me of who I am and my purpose for being here, for who I am is a child of God and my purpose for being here is to share his love to others."

Now I have the confidence to talk to others like me, Wives, mothers, single parents and partners, who go through life with secret abuse from another which is called emotional abuse. Find your strength in the Lord, for with him all things are possible.

You carry me through life's journey
Even when I felt weak and lonely
You carry me when I was weary
And dry the tears when my eyes was teary
I will never doubt your presence
For with you Lord, I cannot be, but with reverence.

The Grace Of God Sustains Me

I can feel the holy spirit, moving within me
I can feel the hand of the angels, holding me
And keeping me from danger, bringing me into
a safe place, where I can think how wonderful
God is, he will protect me.

When I am sad, I cry within but he hears me
And reminds me that he is there
In my distress and sorrows, when I'm fearful
And depressed, fustrated and angry
I can feel the comfort of the holy spirit
Moving within me.

Angels Visit

The Angels in the sky, was slowly going by
In the shape of the clouds
I can see not just one
But that there were three

There they were at the same time
In the dusk, as the sun begins to set at night
As they go by, they seem to say
Everything will be alright

Never doubt when you see
the mystries in the sky
Believe what you feel in your heart
and never ask why, for this you shall know
A gaurdian Angel is going by.

The Heavenly Voice

In my solemn moments when I'm all alone
I will look up in the heavens
And see the clouds rolling by
That fierce clattering sound I hear
It fills so much hearts with fear
Thats when I know he speaks to me.

Behind the dark grey clouds
They are folded in layers
One layer is much lighter than the other
Until I can see an opening through
The milk white clouds, the blue sky
Thats when I know, he speaks to me.

He holds me up and takes care of me
When I'm all alone, he comforts me
He listens when I call to him
And answers with signs unseen
That's when I know he speaks to me.

Never Alone

My hands I can barely feel
My eyes I can hardly open
Even my breath I was struggling to breathe
As I travel alone in the cold
With that wintery breeze, blowing
Right through me
But then I remember how much
God loves me, he will take care of me,
protect me and he will never let me walk alone

Truth

Deep within my heart, my soul has been searching
For the truth
A truth that can open mine eyes to see
and now I know that it shall ever be.

Every thought and every image, so clearly I see
The breath within me is shallow, but oh so free
Hence the day that I've found it
The truth I know shall ever be

The heart that was filled with despair
Will no longer be frail, for
because of the truth
It has set me free

I need You

I need you Lord, with strength from above
I need you Lord, send your angels to me
Give me the strength that I need

Help me to do thy will, please send an angel to me
Send your angel from up above
To show me your love
Oh Lord I need you near, I need you everyday

Teach me to know your will, Do thy will
And to share what your will be done
Each and everyday
For thus you say, your kingdom shall come.

Majestic

You look so beautiful as you rise in the
morning in the east and more glorious
When you set in the west in the evening
You are the best, that no one needs to guess.

You brings such glowing ray of light to many
Throughout the world for all to see
You are the only majestic light that shines so bright
Holy is he who made thee.

My Thoughts

Thy thoughts are quiet, thy moments are silent
Listening to the questions inside my head
Trying to reason with all the answers

Thy thoughts are so deep within
When I look inside, its like an open window
Filled with sunshine, beautiful flowers
And a breath of fresh air

Thy thoughts are wonderful
Filled with hopes and dreams
Nothing can stop thy thoughts
from wondering
For within thy thoughts, my hopes
And dreams keep on believing.

Since I Met Jesus

It was not until I met Jesus
that my life begins to change
It was not until I met Jesus
that I never was the same
It was not until I met you Lord
that my dark clouds have gone
away.
It was not until I met you, Lord Jesus
that all my hearts desire begins to
glow.

Behind That Smile

Behind that smile is a person that is sometimes shy
Behind that smile is a person that is always so kind and true
Behind that smile is a thought that is always so thoughtful
Behind that smile is person that search for the best in others
Behind that smile is a person with a heart that
is filled with love, but now it is smuttered in pain
hoping that one day it is free and happy again
A smile that will last forever, A smile that can reach another.

Serenity Divine

Its such a beautiful place to see
The mountains, the hills so luscious and green
The quiet meadows in the forest, the deep blue sea
The sweet singing birds, the peaceful stream
Its such a love divine, a place of peace and serenity
I close my eyes and breathe a breath of fresh air
and when I open mine eyes in the garden of flowers
they began to open slowly, one flower at a time
the beautiful pink and lavender orchids, the red
hibiscus, the African violets, the pink and yellow
roses, the hyacinth and daffodils.
You can smell their sweet blossoms as they open
up wide.
Oh what a wander of nature such innocent
so soft with tenderness, for all to see.
That place of peace and serenity.

Beautiful Rainbow

Beautiful colours from above
filled the sky with such love
from the north to the south
the east and the west
we can see its beauty, Becuase it is the best.

What do we think, when we look at you
what do we feel or what should we do
Is this the way to show us your love
with that beautiful hug
that comes from up above.
A Rainbow!

My Burdens He Carries

As I travel along with all my sorrows inside,

I would ask myself, for what reason am

I to blame for the mistakes of others.

Why do I need to struggle with a burden of another

when I cannot bare the burden of my own

Then his voice softly said to me,

"Why are you carrying your burden all alone,

it is not for you to bare, talk to me

let me carry your burden for you,
let me be your friend,
So I trusted in him, now I am set free.

Holding On

Hold on to your children each and every day
Give them a hug, teach them the way
The way of the Lord that is mighty and strong
It helps them to know right from wrong.

Hold on to your children each and every day
Give them a hug don't push them away
It teaches them how to love and care
Even when things are dark and despair.

Hold on to your children each and every day
show them you care, lend a listening ear
Hold on to your children, teach them to pray
Teach them to pray each and everyday.

Never Give Up

I could have gave up when my heart was weak
but I did not
I could have gave up when the road seems weary
but I did not
I could have gave up when life seem so empty
with dismay and disappointment
but I did not.

I did not give up
because my God is mighty strong
He gave me strength when my heart was weak
And carry me along that long dreary road
He fills my life with hopes and dreams
With Angels all around me
never more will I feel so empty.

Are You Listening to Me

I am over shadowed by a dark cloud
like the deep blue sea at night
I cried out to the ocean
Can you hear me, can you feel my pain
Are you listening to me ?

The loud waves of emotions rush through me
so many thoughts, so many concerns
so much anguish, so many confusion
help me, I say, help I pray
Are you listening to me

My heart quivers with fear I can feel every beat
rushing through my vein, seems like there's
just one more day, wondering if I go
then what do I say
Are you listening to me.

Down The Road

That lonely road you travel on,
always seems so empty
Longing and searching for someone
to care,
Have you seen him, have you seen
the one along the road

Thy heart is empty, sorrow is mine
Thy soul is searching, is it because
thine heart has been broken
so many mystries in your secret life
how I sit and wonder why

I am confused, is it just me
I am confused, my mind is weak
I thought it was love but it isn't
Oh the pain that I bare
It has been a long lonely road.

A Love Failed

A love that was there but now seems to
be lost, it's because that love no longer
have trust
what is left of love that cannot be healed
Should it be painful, when it seems so real
Sometimes I think it's just a bad deal

Can you see what I see or feel what I feel
The smiles, the charms that I can cease to wonder
Is it real, is it another one of your thrills
How can it be, when life seems so free
but yet it's so hard when face with reallity.

Cries Of A Mirror

When I look at you
I can see a tear of sadness
Oh, how can it be
that lonely look in yours eyes,
that wondering stare, it looks
down the soul inside
I can hear you cry

To not feel that love inside
That love you long for, A love
that is pure and undeniable
to fill that empty void inside
Oh that love, that love, thine
heart yearns for, I can hear you cry

Silently your tear drops fall
Oh how it hurts inside, seeking the love
you once had.
It seems to far to reach, that broken heart
that cries from the mirror on the other side.

Running

Running from the wind and the rain
Running from self, try running again
A self that cannot be regain by your
own strength.
A self that is too selfish to compromise
A self that is so self -contained, it
refused to face reallity
Running from self so selfishly
It's because self by itself
thinks so foolishly.

He Sets Me Free

Look around you what do you see
A world of chaos, a world that is lost
with sadness, despair, hatred and anger

Look around you what do you see
A world that is curious
but yet live with so much animosity
A world that has lost its intergrity

Look around you what do you see
A young heart willing to learn
An old heart wanting to teach

Teaching about love and intergrity
about morals and not immorallity
Teaching about a world that is lost
but soon to be free by the one who died
on the cross for both you and me.

Not Another Child

Little ones with smiling faces
As Angels you've gone to take your places
And even though your stay with us
were just for a short while
A parent heart is comforted
Knowing that you're God's child

So many little ones has lost their lives
Because of the senseless behavior
of another child
Do not take another bullet to an
innocent child
A mothers prayer, A mothers cry
For every child that is in our eyes.

Take up your role as a parent that care
never miss that look or that glaring stare
Remember when you sang them lullaby
Don't let them take up a bullet to another child.

Courage

The test of courage is with one
who is weak but never gave up
One who would fall and continues
to climb
One that would walk through
darkness
but believes that there's a light at
the end.

For great is the one who makes
the effort to believe in one self
and trust in the creator
For only through him
strength will endure to
build on courage and courage
to conquer all fear.

Tribute To My Mother

Mother I want to thank you for all that you have done for me
God has given you the strength of endurance, to teach me
right from wrong.
He gave you a heart of love, to share and
care and you taught me to do
the same.
And for this I do thank you
Mother, if there were times when I failed to listen,
I deeply regret not listening to you,
you were there to show and to guide me
back with a lesson in life and for this I do thank you.
Mother, you have traveled the long dark roads to help put food
on the table and walked millions of miles
to make sure that I was happy
and would cried with tears of sadness when I'm unhappy.
Mother you have walked through the rain and in the sun you
never cease to say it cannot be done, but
continue to strife until it was done
You taught me how to hold my head up high
through trials and tough times,
always pray and let God be my guide.
Mother I thank God for you and for being there for me.
For when he gave me to you, you showed me
how to always be kind and true.
And for this dear Mother again I want to say, "thank you."

The Light

Over the dark blue sea,
streams that light from a distance
it melts the heart with love
that glossy look that glitters around
the hand of God is magically strong

See how the ocean flows
see the wanders around you
his marvellous love
a light that shines from up above
see how the ocean flow with such
glimmer at night, the light
that reflects in the mind.

Quiet as it seems at night
it moves slowly and calmly
with a toug on the ocean floor as
the wind begins to blow
a stream of light that glitters across
that light we all seem to know.

Gentle Water Flows

Through the forest and the hills
The mountains and the valley
flows a stream of living water
that flows down through the willow trees

Listen as the water rolls down the stony brook
and over the rocky hills into an open waterfall
with its misty air so refreshing

The cool flowing water that rustles down the meadows
and through the grassy plains
it calms the heart and soul at night
while sitting under the moonlight.

Imagine This

Have you ever imagine a bird flying
with such trust in the air, I know that God cares
because he is always there.
Have you ever imagine being a butterfly
with colorful wings they fly around with
such ease just enjoying the warm sun
and the cooling breeze
The fragrance is so sweet as you rest
on the flowers.
Can you imagine a world with no flowers
the red, the yellow and all the beautiful
colors.
so pleasing to see the buzzing bee
Oh what a beauty, our eyes will ever see
The wonder of God that will ever be.

The Raging Wind

From across the ocean, she sways along
with a prolonging twirl that continues to blow
Her eyes began to open as she soars through
the trees and houses whistling through
the empty streets
You can hear her howling, blowing
You can feel her strength as it shakes
the structure around us
Her eyes began to open much wider
Everyone is watching, waiting, predicting the
worse, hoping for the best
Her skirt began to spread as she move
further inland
she kept her strength as she made land fall
She made history, in New York and New Jersey
that was the day of hurricane Sandy.

Inspired

I am inspired by the birds
how they soar through the sky
flying high or low as they go by

Nestle in the trees big or small
we listen to the sweet sounds best of all
I am inspired by the birds you see
they're always singing sweet melody.

Listen to the sweet sounds
that you can hear
look for the ones that you can see
touch the ones that you can feel
it's just like magic, placed there for you and me.

I am inspired by the birds
you see,
the ones that can fly so gracefully

Beautiful Grenada

Beautiful Island such beauty I see
The sunshine and the deep blue sea
My beautiful Grenada that feel so free

The papaya and the coconut tree
the white sand and the mango tree
The mountains and the hill tops
so rich and so free
My beautiful Grenada
such beauty I see.

The green grass and the sandy beach
The fisherman by the bayside catching fish
Beautiful Grenada my homeland you'll be
Grenada my Grenada, There's no more like thee.

Be Humble

B   Boast not yourself by the things you do.

E   Effortless should be your kindness to all.

H   Have a sense of humor to help the stress go away.

U   Understand each others differences before making any judgment or two.

M   Morals is important as we live our daily lives.

B   Bring not your burden by yourself.

L   Let go and let God take control of your life.

E   Encourage others to live a life that is without selfishness but with the effect of encouraging one another in benefiting *the good things in life.*

Strength

You gave me strength when I need it most
You gave me courage to face uncertain days
And even when times have change
and my troubles have increased
You showed me Lord that through trails
I need to have faith

Thank you Lord for being there for me
making me who I am
For who I am is a child of God
that see through my eyes all your wonders
And in my heart I keep your words
with faith, hope and love.

Angel Of Light

Standing there by the old oak tree
Is a beautiful angel with its light so bright
The path that I walked through, was so dark with dismay
But at the end there is a guiding light,
That shines for me along the way.

Angel of mercy, come see me through
There's hope I know, when I follow you
For you are my guiding light, I know it's true,
An Angel of light that shines so bright
I know it will also shine for you

Mercy and Mighty

You are the God of mercy and grace
No one can take your place,
you hold us Lord with your mighty hand
And even when we faulter, you didn't laugh or frown
but instead you showed us a better way
you kept holding us strong with your mighty hand

Your Kingdom is great, Your grace is so free,
Lord please be there for me, for I seek your mercy
Do not hide your face from me, O God Almighty
for without you, my strenght would be weak
Lord please hold my hand, for your mercy I seek.

Depending On You Lord

I cried out to you Lord, hear me when I pray
I surrender my soul to you, because I no longer want to go astray
So stressed in many ways, that no one can't imagine
And now I bare my soul out to you Lord
For I can only depend on you.

Nothing dear Lord, will keep me from serving you
Nothing can keep me from calling on you
you carry me through my strife
for you are the gate keeper of my life
you are my strong hold and my rock
My fortress for whom I depend on

Dear Lord I'm depending on you

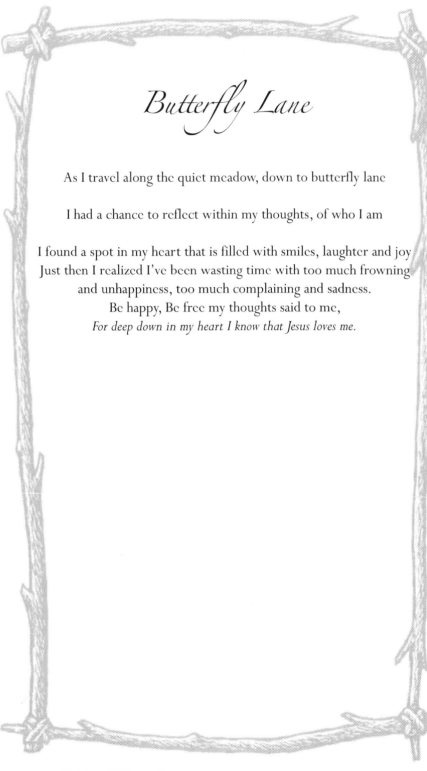

Butterfly Lane

As I travel along the quiet meadow, down to butterfly lane

I had a chance to reflect within my thoughts, of who I am

I found a spot in my heart that is filled with smiles, laughter and joy
Just then I realized I've been wasting time with too much frowning
and unhappiness, too much complaining and sadness.
Be happy, Be free my thoughts said to me,
For deep down in my heart I know that Jesus loves me.

Autobiography

I love writting poetry because it brings me to a place where I can find an inner peace within me and helps me to overcome the things that are stressful in my life, apart from that I love music that inspires me and things of nature.

For great and wonderful is the One who made the heaven and the earth, who cause the waters to flow across the land of the living, who talks through nature around us, who shines the light of sunshine through the day and the moon by night.

For he is the God of Glory and Grace there is no other but him to be Praised.

I was born on the Island of Grenada, also known as the Spice Island.

Grenada is located on the southeastern end of the Grenadines in the Caribbean, it is about 133 sq mls and is approximately 90 mls away from the Island of Trinidad and Tobago. Grenada is famous for its wonderful spices, beautiful white sandy beaches, the nice warm sunshine and smiles of friendly people.

This beautiful Island is consist of six parishes and Two sister Islands, Carriacou and PetiteMartinique.

I was born in the parish of St. David's but at the age of three my family moved to the parish of St. Andrew's where I grew up. I went to high school in the parish of St. Patrick's. I have three wonderful children ages 18, 14 and 5

I work as a restorative coordinator and has dedicate my time and services to help others to find a sense of purpose in their daily lives. My philosophy is to believe in yourself in the things that you do that are good, trust in God always and he will see you through.

Lord when you teach us how to pray
You also teach us how to pray for each other
When the face of God shines down upon us
Lord help us never for a second to doubt who you are
For you guide us along the rough and thorny path and
lead us where the path is clear and free
Satan will try to decieve us
But I know when we let Jesus hold our
hands, he'll never let us go. AMEN